The Essential
CARIBBEAN
COOKBOOK

The Essential CARIBBEAN COOKBOOK

50 CLASSIC RECIPES, WITH STEP-BY-STEP PHOTOGRAPHS

EDITED BY
HEATHER THOMAS

COURAGE
BOOKS

AN IMPRINT OF RUNNING PRESS
PHILADELPHIA • LONDON

© 1998 Reed Consumer Books Limited
First published in the United States in 1998 by Courage Books

Printed in Hong Kong

9 8 7 6 5 4 3 2 1

Digit on the right indicates the number of this printing

Library of Congress Cataloging-in-Publication Number
97-66808

ISBN 0-7624-0277-6

Designed and produced by SP Creative Design
Wickham Skeith, Suffolk, England
Editor and writer: Heather Thomas
Art director: Al Rockall
Designer: Rolando Ugolini
Special photography: Steve Baxter
Step-by-step photography: GGS Photographics, Norwich
Food preparation: Meg Jansz and Caroline Stevens
Produced by Mandarin Offset

Published by Courage Books, an imprint of
Running Press Book Publishers
125 South Twenty-second Street
Philadelphia, Pennsylvania 19103-4399

Notes

1. Standard spoon measurements are used in all recipes.

2. Eggs should be large unless otherwise stated.

3. Whole milk should be used unless otherwise stated.

4. Fresh herbs should be used unless otherwise stated.
If unavailable, use dried herbs as an alternative, but halve
the quantities stated.

CONTENTS

INTRODUCTION

There are over 200 islands in the thin chain that stretches for 2,600 miles from Florida in the north to Venezuela in the south. To the east of these islands lie the turbulent waters of the Atlantic Ocean, whereas to the west they are lapped by the calmer, clear waters of the warm Caribbean Sea. The islands are still a fascinating melting pot of different people, each with their own traditions, culture, and culinary heritage.

The food they eat, its preparation and presentation, reflects the diversity of their origins. Many dishes can be traced back to the cooking of the Caribs and Arawaks, the islands' original inhabitants, as well as to the British, Spanish, Dutch, French, and, of course, the Africans who brought their own ingredients and cooking skills when they were transported to the islands to work on the vast new sugar plantations. In the nineteenth century, Indian and Chinese immigrants arrived in Trinidad, bringing with them a love of hot, spicy food, curries and rice dishes, and these too have now become an intrinsic part of Caribbean cooking.

Exotic fruits, tropical vegetables, spices, and seafood are abundant, and all contribute to the unique cuisine of the islands. Most savory dishes are highly seasoned with freshly picked spices, hot pepper sauces, garlic, and coconut. If you visit the markets in the small towns, you will see piles of huge golden pumpkins, bundles of hot chiles, fibrous coconuts, gigantic dark green callaloo leaves, fists of black plantains, and the ubiquitous yams, sweet potatoes, cassava, breadfruit, okra, and christophenes, alongside clay cooking pots and local basketware.

The old women have an enticing array of spices for sale: fresh nutmegs in their delicate filigree of crimson mace, bundles of aromatic cinnamon bark, little bags of allspice berries, cloves, and black peppercorns, and crumbling cocoa sticks. To experience the real atmosphere of the Caribbean and to sample the native foods, you must visit one of these colorful, bustling markets or eat at one of the many roadside stands or family-run rum shacks. This is where the best and most authentic Caribbean food is usually to be discovered, far away from the tourist beaches and hotels.

Allspice

These dark brown berries resemble black peppercorns and come from an evergreen tree in the bay family. Sometimes known as pimento or Jamaica pepper, they can be used whole or ground. They have a very distinctive flavor, which is reminiscent of cinnamon, cloves, juniper berries, and nutmeg. Allspice berries are particularly popular in Jamaica, where "jerked" meat and chicken are often grilled over allspice branches to impart more flavor to the finished dish.

Bananas

There are many varieties of banana in the Caribbean, ranging from small red and yellow-skinned ones to the large black plantains. Green bananas may be cooked and served as a savory dish, whereas

yellow ones may be eaten as a snack or dessert. Thus bananas are boiled, fried, curried, grilled, baked, and stuffed. You will find recipes for many of these dishes in this book. Banana leaves also have their uses and make a good substitute for kitchen foil when wrapping and cooking food.

Callaloo

These are the gigantic green spreading leaves of the dasheen, eddo, or taro plant, which grows in the tropical rainforests of the Caribbean. When cooked, they resemble spinach, and have given their name to the islands' most famous soup.

Chayotes

This pale green, pear-shaped vegetable is also known as christophene or cho-cho. It has a delicate flavor, which is similar to that of marrow, and a distinctively crisp texture. In the Caribbean, it is served baked, stuffed, boiled, or even dressed in salads. Christophenes are usually boiled in their skins, although they may be peeled before cooking.

Chiles

There are many different varieties of chiles, all with exotic names like bird peppers and Scotch bonnets. They originated in Mexico and were brought to the Caribbean by the Spanish. The hottest chiles of all are the Scotch bonnets, beloved of the Jamaicans, and these are pale green, red, or yellow. They

are added to many dishes, immersed in oils, or crushed with vinegar and made into the hot sauces which appear on every Caribbean dinner table.

Cilantro

This pungent herb is used extensively in the Spanish-speaking islands of the Caribbean. The leaves are used for flavoring savory dishes, whereas the seeds are ground as a spice.

Cinnamon

These scented bark quills come from the inner bark of the cinnamon tree, which grows widely in Grenada and some of the other islands. In the Caribbean, cinnamon is always sold in its bark form, tied into rough bundles, and then it can be ground into powder as required.

Cloves

These are actually unopened flower buds, and they may be purchased either whole or ground. For maximum strength and aroma, it is always best to grind them yourself before adding to a dish.

Coconuts

The coconut has so many culinary and practical uses in the Caribbean. It may be split open and the coconut water consumed as a refreshing drink; or the water may be mixed with the grated flesh to make coconut milk. This is added to many classic savory and sweet dishes. The coconut flesh is also used in cooking, while the fibrous outer coating of the coconut is used for weaving floor and wall coverings.

Conch

Most people are more familiar with the beautiful pearly pink shell of this mollusc than the meat inside. It is considered a great delicacy throughout the Caribbean, and is thought to be an aphrodisiac. Indeed, young men are encouraged to eat conch to improve their virility. Before cooking, conch (pronounced "conk") is beaten to tenderize it. Likewise, it is important to avoid over-cooking or it may be very rubbery and tough. It is difficult to obtain fresh conch outside of the Caribbean, although it can be bought in cans in many West Indian specialist shops.

Limes

It is hard to imagine Caribbean food without limes. They are used in so many dishes, both sweet and savory, as well as in drinks and punches. Limes are a tropical citrus fruit and cannot be grown successfully in more temperate and Mediterranean climates. When buying limes, always choose fresh, plump ones, and avoid any wrinkled or dry-looking fruit. Limes go well with chicken and fish dishes; often the juice is added to marinades, sauces, and basting mixtures.

Molasses

These are a by-product of refining sugar cane. Dark brown, almost black, in color, they have long been used in the West Indies as a natural sweetening agent. With their subtly spicy flavor, they have a natural affinity with bananas and fruit.

Nutmeg

Nutmeg and mace are widely used spices which both come from the same tree. The aromatic nutmeg is encapsulated in a tough dark outer casing which, in turn, is wrapped in a filigree of crimson mace. As it ages, the mace fades from bright red to a dull golden color. Nutmeg is always at its most pungent when grated fresh rather than using the ground powder you can buy packaged in stores. In the Caribbean it is used for flavoring soups, curries, desserts, and drinks.

Okra

This pale green, spear-shaped vegetable was imported from Africa and is now an essential ingredient in many Caribbean dishes. It is added to many soups, stews, sauces and curries and has a thickening quality. However, it also tends to be rather slimey and sticky in texture when cooked. You can combat the worst of the stickiness by washing and drying the okra pods before cooking. Okra is also known as ladyfingers or gumbo.

Pepper sauces

No West Indian table would be complete without the requisite bottle of hot pepper sauce, and every island has its own speciality. These sauces range from fiery reds through shades of orange to golds and yellows. They are used as a seasoning for most dishes, but do take care when using them as they can be incredibly hot!

Plantains

These resemble large bananas, and when unripe (green) or semi-ripe (yellow) they are cooked as a starchy vegetable or added to stews and savory dishes. Their skin turns black as they ripen and they may then be used in desserts. Plantains are never eaten raw; they are always cooked.

Rum

The distilled spirit of sugar cane or molasses is used in many classic West Indian sweet and savory dishes as well as in drinks, especially the world-famous rum punch and planter's punch. Rums vary considerably in their flavor and quality, and while some are very rough and unrefined, others are on a par with the finest French brandies.

Saltfish

Salted cod was originally the staple food of slaves working on the plantations, but it is now considered a delicacy and has become Jamaica's national dish. It should always be washed thoroughly and soaked overnight in several changes of water before using.

Sweet potatoes

These starchy vegetables are eaten widely throughout the islands, and are used in both sweet and savory dishes. The flesh may be orange, yellow or white, while the skins are red or orange. Always buy whole, uncut sweet potatoes and handle them very gently. They can be boiled or baked in their skins, or they may be mashed like ordinary potatoes.

Yams

These edible tubers are similar to potatoes, but have a nuttier flavor. Yams originated in Africa and were brought to the West Indies by the African slaves. Despite their unprepossessing appearance, they are revered by West Indian cooks and may be boiled, grilled over hot coals, or broiled.

Cooking utensils

Traditional Caribbean cooking utensils are rustic and practical. They can be bought in local markets alongside the fruit and vegetables on display. However, all the dishes in this book can be cooked with conventional modern Western cookware if you cannot obtain the authentic pots and dishes.

Canarees: these are earthenware casserole and pie dishes.

Coalpots: these are traditional iron or clay pots which are perfect for slow-cooked dishes, such as pepperpots.

Pestle and mortar: large or small, these are commonly used for grinding spices and pounding foods.

Yabbas: these glazed clay pots are used for storage, mixing, and cooking.

SOUPE GERMOU

Pumpkin soup (St Lucia)

4 tablespoons butter
2 onions, finely chopped
1 garlic clove, chopped
2-pound wedge of pumpkin
1 large tomato, skinned, seeded, and chopped
2 sprigs of parsley
1 bay leaf
5 cups chicken broth
pinch of sugar
salt and freshly ground black pepper
1 cup light cream
dash of hot pepper sauce

To garnish:

chopped chives
grated fresh nutmeg

1 Melt the butter in a large saucepan over low heat. Add the onions and garlic and stir well. Cook slowly in the butter until the onions are soft and golden, but take care that they do not brown.

3 Add the chicken broth, sugar, and seasoning. Cover the pan and simmer gently over low heat for 30 to 40 minutes, until the pumpkin starts to break up into the soup. Remove the parsley and bay leaf and then purée the soup in a food processor or blender until smooth.

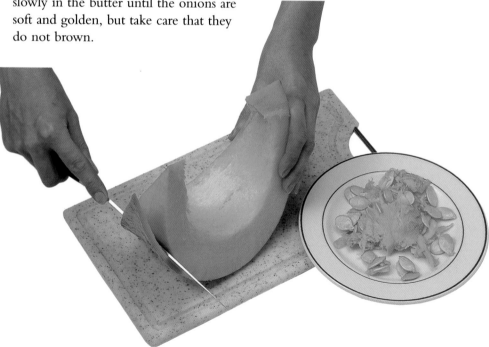

2 While the onions are cooking, remove the rind, seeds, and any stringy bits from the pumpkin and cut the flesh into small chunks. Add to the onions in the pan with the tomato and herbs, and sauté for 2 to 3 minutes.

PREPARATION: 10 MINUTES
COOKING: 45 TO 55 MINUTES
SERVES: 6

4 Return the puréed soup to the pan and stir in the cream and hot pepper sauce. Check the seasoning and then heat through gently. Serve in bowls garnished with chives and grated nutmeg.

CALLALOO

Barbados

1 Wash the callaloo or spinach leaves thoroughly under running cold water to remove any dirt. Drain, shake dry, and then chop them, cutting out and discarding any hard stems.

2 Heat the peanut oil in a large saucepan and add the onion, scallions, and garlic. Fry gently for 5 minutes, or until softened. Add the red chile, turmeric, and thyme, and stir over low heat for 1 to 2 minutes.

PREPARATION: 15 MINUTES
COOKING: 35 MINUTES
SERVES: 6

3 Stir in the okra and then add the chopped callaloo or spinach leaves. Turn up the heat and cook, stirring, until the leaves start to wilt. Reduce the heat and add the chicken broth and saffron. Bring to the boil, and then cover and simmer for 20 minutes.

1 pound fresh callaloo or spinach leaves
3 tablespoons peanut oil
1 large onion, finely chopped
4 scallions, chopped
2 garlic cloves, crushed
1 fresh red chile, seeded and finely chopped
1 teaspoon turmeric
sprig of thyme, crumbled
8 ounces okra, sliced thinly
3³/4 cups chicken broth
few strands of saffron
1³/4 cups coconut milk
1 cup crabmeat, fresh or canned
salt and freshly ground black pepper
juice of ¹/2 lime
dash of hot pepper sauce

4 Add the coconut milk and crabmeat and stir well. Heat gently for 4 to 5 minutes and then season to taste with salt and pepper. Just before serving, stir in the lime juice and hot pepper sauce.

PEPPERPOT SOUP

Jamaica

2 pounds lean beef
8 ounces lean pork
7$^{1}/_{2}$ cups water
1 pound spring cabbage, chopped
1 pound callaloo or spinach leaves, washed and chopped
1 onion, chopped
2 green bell peppers, seeded and chopped
2 scallions, chopped
8 ounces yam, peeled and sliced
1 large potato, sliced
1 sprig of thyme
1 garlic clove, crushed
24 okra, trimmed and sliced
2 tablespoons butter
$^{5}/_{8}$ cup coconut milk
salt and freshly ground black pepper

For the dumplings:

2$^{1}/_{4}$ cups flour
pinch of salt
2 teaspoons baking powder
2 tablespoons margarine

1 Trim any fat from the beef and pork and cut the meat into cubes. Place in a large saucepan with the water and bring to the boil. Reduce the heat, cover the pan, and simmer gently for 45 minutes.

3 While the soup is cooking, make the dumplings. Sift the flour, salt, and baking powder into a bowl and rub in the margarine. Add sufficient water to mix to a stiff dough. Knead until soft and smooth and shape into 18 balls. Flatten them and cook in salted boiling water for 10 minutes.

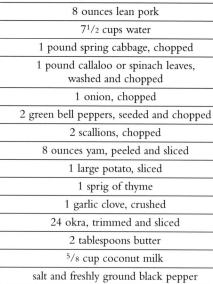

2 Add the spring cabbage with the callaloo or spinach leaves, onion, green bell peppers, scallions, yam, potato, thyme, and garlic. Simmer gently in the covered pan for 15 to 30 minutes, until the vegetables are tender and the meat is cooked.

PREPARATION: 30 MINUTES
COOKING: 1$^{1}/_{4}$ HOURS
SERVES: 6

4 In a skillet, fry the okra in the butter until golden brown on both sides. Remove and drain. Add to the soup with the coconut milk and simmer for 5 minutes. Season to taste and serve in individual bowls with the hot dumplings.

FISH SOUP

Guadeloupe

1 Put the fish heads, bones, and trimmings in a large saucepan with the water. Shell the shrimp, and add the heads, tails, and shells to the fish trimmings in the pan with the black peppercorns and bay leaf. Reserve the shelled shrimp.

2 Place the pan over high heat and bring to the boil. Reduce the heat and cover the pan, and then simmer gently for 30 minutes. Strain the fish broth through into a large bowl and set aside.

3 Heat the oil in a large saucepan and add the onion, garlic, and green bell pepper. Sauté until the onion is softened and golden. Add the scallions and tomatoes and continue cooking for 2 minutes, stirring.

1 pound filleted white fish, plus heads, bones, and trimmings
7¹/₂ cups water
1¹/₂ cups cooked shrimp
4 whole black peppercorns
1 bay leaf
3 tablespoons oil
1 large onion, chopped
2 garlic cloves, crushed
1 small green bell pepper, seeded and chopped
3 scallions, chopped
3 tomatoes, skinned, seeded, and chopped
¹/₄ teaspoon saffron powder
strip of lime zest
2 cloves
2 allspice berries
salt and freshly ground black pepper
dash of lime juice

PREPARATION: 15 MINUTES
COOKING: 1 HOUR 10 MINUTES
SERVES: 6

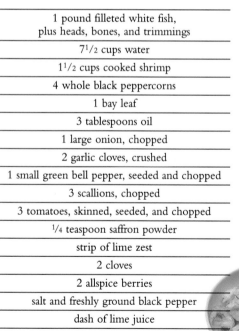

4 Add the reserved fish broth, saffron, lime zest, cloves, and allspice berries. Bring to the boil and then reduce the heat and simmer for 15 minutes. Add the white fish fillets and shrimp and cook gently for 10 minutes. Season to taste and add a dash of lime juice. Serve hot.

CHILLED AVOCADO SOUP
Bahamas

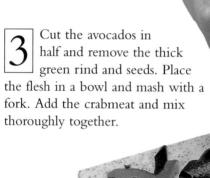

3 Cut the avocados in half and remove the thick green rind and seeds. Place the flesh in a bowl and mash with a fork. Add the crabmeat and mix thoroughly together.

1 Melt the butter in a large saucepan over low heat. Add the onion and garlic and stir well. Cook gently, without coloring, until the onion is soft and translucent.

4 tablespoons butter
1 onion, finely chopped
1 garlic clove, crushed
1 tablespoon flour
5 cups chicken broth
4 ripe avocados
1 cup crabmeat, fresh or canned
1¹/₄ cups light cream
salt and freshly ground black pepper
To garnish:
sliced avocado
snipped chives or cilantro

2 Stir in the flour and cook gently, stirring continuously, for 1 to 2 minutes. Do not allow the flour to brown. Add the chicken broth, a little at a time, and continue stirring until the flour is mixed in thoroughly and the liquid is smooth and free from lumps. Bring to the boil and then reduce the heat.

PREPARATION: 10 MINUTES +
CHILLING TIME
COOKING: 30 TO 35 MINUTES
SERVES: 6

4 Add the mashed avocado and the crabmeat to the soup and simmer gently for 15 to 20 minutes. Stir in the cream and season to taste with salt and pepper. Remove from the heat and let cool. Cover and then chill in the refrigerator. Serve chilled, garnished with sliced avocado and chives or cilantro.

ACRATS DE MORUE
Salted codfish fritters (Guadeloupe)

2 Put the salted codfish in a bowl and cover with warm water. Set aside to soak for 2 to 3 hours. During this time, you should change the water at least twice. Drain the fish well, and then remove the skin and bones.

1 Make the batter: sift the flour into a bowl. Beat the eggs with the melted butter and then add to the flour. Beat well and then gradually beat in the milk, a little at a time. If the batter is too stiff, thin it with a little more milk. Cover and set aside for 2 to 3 hours.

1½ cups flour
2 eggs
3 tablespoons butter, melted and cooled
1 cup milk
8 ounces salted codfish
1 fresh red chile, seeded and finely chopped
2 scallions, finely chopped
1 garlic clove, crushed
1 tablespoon chopped parsley
½ teaspoon dried thyme
salt and freshly ground black pepper
oil for deep-frying
hot pepper sauce, to serve

3 Flake the fish and place in a mortar with the chile, scallions, garlic, herbs, and seasoning. Pound until smooth. Alternatively, purée in a blender or food processor. Mix into the batter and let stand for 30 minutes.

4 Heat the oil in a deep-fryer or heavy saucepan to 375°F. Drop spoonfuls of the fish mixture into the oil and fry in batches until golden all over. Remove with a perforated spoon and drain on paper towels. Serve hot with hot pepper sauce.

PREPARATION: 15 MINUTES +
STANDING + SOAKING TIME
COOKING: 5 TO 10 MINUTES
SERVES: 6

HONEYED CHICKEN WINGS

Grenadines

3 tablespoons soy sauce

4 tablespoons liquid honey

2 tablespoons vinegar

1 tablespoon sherry

2 teaspoons soft brown sugar

1/2 teaspoon ground ginger

1 garlic clove, crushed

12 chicken wings, trimmed

For the dipping sauce:

2 tablespoons shredded onion

2 tablespoons olive oil

2 tablespoons brown sugar

1 teaspoon lime juice

2 tablespoons peanut butter

6 tablespoons coconut cream

pinch of salt

2 Put the chicken wings in a shallow bowl and pour the honey marinade over the top. Smear the marinade all over the wings, then cover and leave in a cool place to marinate for 2 hours.

1 Put the soy sauce, honey, vinegar, sherry, sugar, ginger, and garlic in a bowl and mix well together, blending thoroughly until smooth.

PREPARATION: 15 MINUTES +
MARINATING TIME
COOKING: 15 TO 20 MINUTES
SERVES: 4

3 While the wings are marinating, make the sauce. Fry the onion in the oil for about 5 minutes until golden brown. Stir in the sugar, lime juice, and peanut butter, and then add the coconut cream, a little at a time. Add the salt and cook over gentle heat until smooth and thick. Set aside.

4 Remove the chicken wings from the marinade and place on a rack in a baking pan. Cook in a preheated oven at 375°F for 15 to 20 minutes, until crisp and golden brown and cooked through. Baste from time to time with any leftover marinade. Alternatively, broil over hot coals or grill for 5 to 7 minutes each side. Serve with the warm peanut dipping sauce.

RUN DOWN
Jamaica

1 pound mackerel or other small fish
juice of 1 lime
3³/₄ cups coconut milk
1 onion, shredded
1 garlic clove, crushed
2 green bell peppers, seeded and chopped
1 fresh red chile, seeded and finely chopped
3 tomatoes, skinned and chopped
2 teaspoons chopped thyme
2 teaspoons chopped chives
1 tablespoon malt vinegar
salt and freshly ground black pepper

1 Clean and scale the mackerel and then remove the bones and fillet them. Put them in a bowl and pour the lime juice over the top. Set aside in a cool place.

4 Add the marinaded mackerel fillets and lime juice, and continue cooking gently until the fish is cooked and tender. Serve with fried bananas as a first course.

2 Pour the coconut milk into a deep, heavy-based skillet. Bring the coconut milk to the boil and continue boiling for about 15 minutes, until it becomes oily.

PREPARATION: 15 MINUTES
COOKING: 35 MINUTES
SERVES: 4

3 Add the onion, garlic, green bell peppers, and chile and cook gently for about 5 minutes, until the onion is softened but not brown. Add the tomatoes, thyme, chives, and vinegar and stir well. Cook gently over low heat for 10 minutes. Season to taste.

ROTI

Curried snacks (Trinidad)

2¹/₄ cups flour

¹/₂ teaspoon baking soda

pinch of salt

4 to 5 tablespoons milk

clarified butter for frying

For the filling:

Colombo de Porc (see page 58) or
Curried Shrimp (see page 44)

1 Sift the flour, baking soda, and salt into a bowl. Bind together with enough milk to form a stiff dough. Knead lightly with your hands and transfer to a lightly floured surface.

3 Heat a griddle and cook the roti until lightly browned on both sides, turning them frequently during cooking. Keep brushing them with a little clarified butter to prevent them sticking.

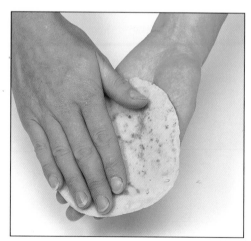

2 With floured hands, divide the dough into 8 pieces and then roll into balls, about the size of an egg. Flatten them out and spread with a little clarified butter, and then pat back to an egg shape again before flattening them once more. Let stand for 30 minutes.

4 Remove the roti from the griddle and place in the palm of one hand. Clap your hands together around the roti several times. You can use a cloth to prevent burning your hands. Fill the roti with Colombo de Porc or Curried Shrimp and roll up.

PREPARATION: 10 MINUTES +
STANDING TIME
COOKING: 10 MINUTES
MAKES: 8

ESCOVITCH

Pickled fish (Jamaica)

2 In the oil remaining in the pan, fry the white fish fillets until they are lightly browned on both sides, turning once. Lift out the fillets and arrange them in a large serving dish. Place the onions and bell peppers on top of the fish.

1 Heat 4 tablespoons of the oil in a large, heavy skillet and add the onions and bell peppers. Fry over gentle heat until the onions are tender and golden and the bell peppers are soft. Remove and set aside.

6 tablespoons olive oil
2 onions, thinly sliced
2 green bell peppers, seeded and sliced
2 pounds white fish fillets
$1^{7}/_{8}$ cups water
1 bay leaf
1-inch piece fresh gingerroot, peeled and chopped
6 peppercorns
$^{1}/_{8}$ teaspoon mace
salt and freshly ground black pepper
$^{5}/_{8}$ cup vinegar
To garnish:
black olives
sweet red pimientos

PREPARATION: 10 MINUTES
COOKING: 25 TO 30 MINUTES
SERVES: 8 (AS A FIRST COURSE)

3 Put the water in a saucepan with the bay leaf, ginger, peppercorns, and mace. Season with salt and pepper and simmer gently for 15 minutes. Add the remaining olive oil and the vinegar and simmer for 2 more minutes.

4 Strain the liquid and discard the bay leaf and spices. Pour the strained liquid over the fish fillets, onions, and bell peppers. This dish can either be served hot, or it can be cooled and then chilled before serving cold. Garnish with black olives and pimientos.

DAUBE DE POISSONS
Tuna in tomato sauce (Martinique)

1 Put the tuna steaks in a shallow dish. Blend together the lime juice, garlic, chile, and salt, and sprinkle over the tuna steaks. Pour the water over the top and leave to marinade in a cool place for 1 to 2 hours.

2 Drain the tuna and throw away the marinade. Dredge the tuna with flour and then fry in the oil in a large skillet until golden brown on both sides. Remove from the skillet and keep warm while you make the sauce.

3 Add the onion, scallions, and red bell pepper to the oil in the skillet and fry gently until softened. Stir in the tomatoes and add the bay leaf, thyme, seasoning, and wine or water. Simmer gently for a few minutes.

4 tuna steaks
juice of 2 limes
2 garlic cloves, crushed
1 fresh red chile, seeded and crushed
pinch of salt
1¼ cups water
flour for dredging
3 tablespoons olive oil
1 onion, finely chopped
3 scallions, chopped
1 red bell pepper, seeded and chopped
3 tomatoes, skinned and chopped
1 bay leaf
sprig of fresh thyme
salt and freshly ground black pepper
4 tablespoons dry white wine or water
To serve:
juice of ½ lime
1 tablespoon olive oil
lime wedges

4 Add the tuna steaks to the tomato sauce in the skillet. Cover and continue cooking gently for 10 minutes, or until the tuna is cooked. Stir in the lime juice and olive oil, and serve immediately with lime wedges.

PREPARATION: 10 MINUTES
+ MARINATING TIME
COOKING: 25 MINUTES
SERVES: 4

SPICY BAKED FISH

Windward Islands

1 (3-pound) striped bass (or large white fish), cleaned and scaled

juice of 2 limes

salt and freshly ground black pepper

1 onion, thinly sliced

6 tablespoons olive oil

For the stuffing:

2 cups soft bread crumbs

4 tablespoons butter, melted

1 tablespoon finely chopped chives

1 teaspoon finely chopped cilantro

1 green bell pepper, seeded and finely chopped

½ onion, shredded

grated rind and juice of 1 lime

pinch of grated nutmeg

salt and freshly ground black pepper

For the topping:

2 tablespoons oil

1 small onion, chopped

1 garlic clove, crushed

1 fresh red chile, seeded and chopped

1 tablespoon chopped cilantro

4 tablespoons fish broth

1 Make the stuffing: put the bread crumbs in a bowl and mix in the melted butter and all the remaining ingredients. Blend well and then set aside to cool.

2 Wash and dry the fish and place in a large dish. Sprinkle it with the lime juice and season inside and out. Set aside in a cool place for about 1 hour to marinate.

PREPARATION: 25 MINUTES
+ MARINATING TIME
COOKING: 30 TO 40
MINUTES

3 Make the topping: heat the oil in a skillet and add the onion and garlic. Fry gently until the onion is softened and golden. Add the chile and continue cooking for 2 to 3 minutes. Stir in the cilantro and fish broth.

4 Remove the fish from the marinade and fill it with the stuffing. Secure with skewers or toothpicks. Arrange the sliced onion in a large ovenproof dish and place the fish on top. Pour over the oil and any remaining marinade, and scatter the topping mixture over the fish. Bake in a preheated oven at 350°F for 30 to 40 minutes.

POISSON EN BLAFF

Creole poached fish (Guadeloupe)

1 Wash, clean, and scale the red snappers, leaving the heads and tails on. Pat the fish dry with paper towels and then place it in a shallow bowl.

2 Make the marinade: mix together the lime juice, crushed allspice, and garlic with the seasoning and chopped chile. Pour over the fish and leave to marinate in a cool place for 1 hour.

PREPARATION: 10 MINUTES +
MARINATING TIME
COOKING: 10 TO 15 MINUTES
SERVES: 4

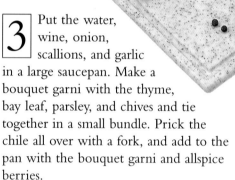

3 Put the water, wine, onion, scallions, and garlic in a large saucepan. Make a bouquet garni with the thyme, bay leaf, parsley, and chives and tie together in a small bundle. Prick the chile all over with a fork, and add to the pan with the bouquet garni and allspice berries.

4 small red snappers
2½ cups water
⅝ cup dry white wine
1 small onion, sliced
3 scallions, chopped
1 garlic clove, peeled
1 sprig of fresh thyme
1 bay leaf
1 sprig of parsley
a few chives
1 fresh red chile
2 allspice berries
For the marinade:
juice of 4 limes
2 allspice berries, crushed
2 garlic cloves, crushed
salt and freshly ground black pepper
1 fresh red chile, seeded and finely chopped

4 Bring to the boil and then add the marinated fish. When the liquid returns to the boil, reduce the heat and simmer for 5 to 10 minutes, until cooked. Discard the bouquet garni. Remove the fish and serve in bowls with the poaching liquid ladled over the top. Serve with rice and fried bananas.

FISH WITH HOT PEPPER SAUCE
St Lucia

1 Make the hot pepper sauce: heat the peanut oil in a saucepan and add the onions and garlic. Fry over medium heat until softened and golden brown. Add the chiles and allspice berries, and continue cooking for 3 to 4 minutes. Set aside to cool a little.

2 Put the onion and spice mixture in a blender or food processor and process for 1 minute. Remove and then blend in the seasoning, lime juice, and vinegar.

4 Heat the oil in a large skillet and add the tuna steaks. Fry on both sides until cooked and golden brown. Remove and drain on paper towels and then serve with the hot pepper sauce. Take care not to use too much sauce as it is very hot. Leftover sauce can be stored for a few days in the refrigerator.

3 Place the tuna steaks in a bowl and pour over the lime juice and a little salt, rubbing it in well. Dredge them with flour and then dip them first into the beaten egg and then the bread crumbs, coating them well.

PREPARATION: 20 MINUTES
COOKING: 15 MINUTES
SERVES: 4

4 thick fish steaks, e.g. tuna
juice of 2 limes
salt
flour for dredging
1 egg, beaten
bread crumbs for coating
oil for shallow-frying
For the hot pepper sauce:
2 tablespoons peanut oil
2 onions, finely chopped
2 garlic cloves, chopped
12 fresh red chiles, seeded and finely chopped
2 allspice berries, crushed
salt and freshly ground black pepper
juice of 1 lime
5 tablespoons vinegar

FISH CURRY

Barbados

3 tablespoons butter

1 large onion, finely chopped

1 garlic clove, crushed

1 tablespoon curry powder

1 tablespoon flour

1¾ cups coconut milk

½ fresh green chile, seeded and chopped

1¼ pounds white fish fillets

juice of ½ lime

salt and freshly ground black pepper

To garnish:

chopped cilantro

3 While the curry sauce is cooking, skin the white fish fillets with a sharp knife. Discard the skin and arrange the fillets in a shallow ovenproof dish. Squeeze the lime juice over the top.

1 Melt the butter in a heavy skillet over low heat, taking care that it does not brown. Add the onion and garlic and then cook gently until softened and golden.

2 Add the curry powder and flour and stir well. Cook gently over very low heat for 2 minutes, stirring. Add the coconut milk and chile, and stir well to mix them thoroughly. Simmer gently over low heat for 5 to 10 minutes, until smooth and thickened.

4 Season the curry sauce and pour over the fish fillets. Cover the dish and cook in a preheated oven at 325°F for 12-15 minutes, until the fish is just cooked but still firm. Garnish with a sprinkling of cilantro and serve with boiled rice and some mango chutney.

PREPARATION: 10 MINUTES
COOKING: 25 TO 30 MINUTES
SERVES: 4

CURRIED SHRIMP PILAU

Tobago

1 pound uncooked jumbo shrimp
juice of 2 limes
4 tablespoons peanut oil
1 large onion, chopped
2 garlic cloves, crushed
1 fresh red chile, seeded and finely chopped
1 green bell pepper, seeded and chopped
2 to 3 teaspoons curry powder
1½ cups long-grain rice
3 cups coconut milk
salt and freshly ground black pepper

To garnish:

chopped cilantro
whole cooked shrimp
fresh red chiles

1 Shell the shrimp, removing the heads, shells, legs, and tails. Take out the black intestinal vein running along the back. Put the shelled shrimp in a bowl and sprinkle the lime juice over the top. Set aside to marinade while you make the pilau.

3 Add the rice and stir well until all the grains are glistening with oil. Pour in the coconut milk and mix well. Cover the skillet and cook over very low heat for 15-20 minutes, until the rice is tender and all the liquid has been absorbed. Check the rice occasionally, stirring to prevent it sticking. Add more liquid if necessary.

4 Add the shrimp and their lime juice marinade to the rice, stirring through to distribute them evenly. Season to taste with salt and pepper, and heat through gently. Serve hot garnished with cilantro, shrimp, and chiles.

2 Heat the peanut oil in a large, deep skillet and add the onion, garlic, chile, and green bell pepper. Fry gently until the onion and pepper are softened but not brown. Stir in the curry powder and cook for 2 to 3 minutes.

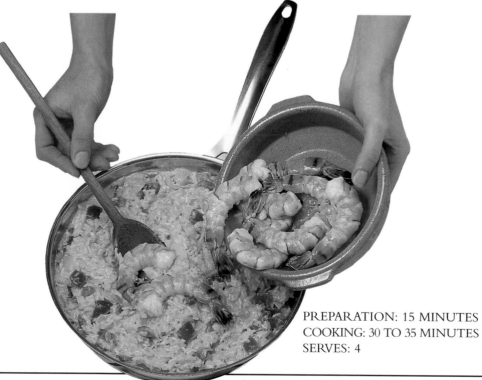

PREPARATION: 15 MINUTES
COOKING: 30 TO 35 MINUTES
SERVES: 4

CRAB CREOLE
Martinique

1 Remove the crab claws and legs and crack them to extract the meat. Open the crabs by pressing with your thumbs on the edge of the section of the shell to which the legs were attached. Pull out the central section.

2 Discard the stomach sac and feathery gills. Scoop out the meat from inside the shell and put in a bowl with the meat from the claws and legs. Remove the meat from the leg sockets with a skewer and mix with the other crabmeat. Mash well with a fork.

| 4 medium-sized cooked crabs |
| 1½ cups bread crumbs |
| 2 red bell peppers, seeded and finely chopped |
| 1 garlic clove, crushed |
| 1 fresh red chile, seeded and finely chopped |
| pinch of ground mace |
| ½ teaspoon ground allspice berries |
| 2 tablespoons chopped parsley |
| juice of 1 lime |
| 2 tablespoons rum (optional) |
| salt and freshly ground black pepper |
| 1 tablespoon butter |

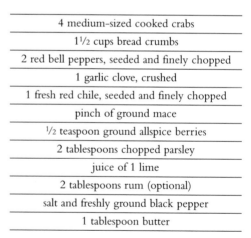

PREPARATION: 25 MINUTES
COOKING: 30 MINUTES
SERVES: 4

3 Add 1 cup of the bread crumbs to the crabmeat, together with the red bell peppers, garlic, chile, mace, allspice, and parsley. Add the lime juice and rum (if using) and season with salt and pepper.

4 Scrub and wash the empty crab shells and fill with the crabmeat stuffing mixture. Sprinkle with the remaining bread crumbs and dot with butter. Bake in a preheated oven at 350°F for 30 minutes, until browned.

CURRIED SHRIMP IN PINEAPPLE

Trinidad

1½ pounds uncooked shrimp
juice of 1 lime
2 tablespoons vegetable oil
1 onion, finely chopped
1 tablespoon chopped chives
2 tomatoes, skinned and chopped
2 tablespoons curry powder
1¼ cups fish broth or water
2 tablespoons butter, softened
3 tablespoons flour
2 small pineapples
chopped chives, to garnish

1 Shell the shrimp and remove the black intestinal vein running along the back of each shrimp. Place the shrimp in a bowl, sprinkle with the lime juice and set aside.

3 Add the fish broth or water and the shrimp and stir well. Simmer over low heat for 15 minutes. Remove the skillet from the heat. Blend the butter and flour together and add in small pieces to the shrimp curry, stirring until thickened and smooth. Cook gently for 3 more minutes.

4 Plunge the pineapples into boiling water for 3 minutes and then drain. Cut them in half lengthwise and hollow out some of the flesh. Spoon the curried shrimp mixture into the hollowed-out pineapples and sprinkle with chives.

2 Heat the oil in a heavy skillet and add the onion and chives. Cook gently for about 5 minutes until the onion is softened. Add the tomatoes and curry powder and continue cooking over low heat for about 5 minutes, stirring frequently.

PREPARATION:
15 MINUTES
COOKING: 30 MINUTES
SERVES: 4

SHRIMP WITH MANGO SAUCE

St Lucia

1½ pounds uncooked jumbo shrimp
1 cup flour
pinch of salt
1 tablespoon olive oil
1 egg, separated
⅝ cup coconut milk
oil for deep-frying
For the mango sauce:
4 large ripe mangoes
4 tablespoons water
3 tablespoons sugar
pinch of ground ginger
pinch of ground cinnamon
1 teaspoon curry powder
juice of ½ lime
pinch of salt

3 Make the mango sauce: peel the mangoes and remove the pits. Cut up the flesh and process in a blender or food processor. Put the purée in a saucepan, add the water and stir over low heat until blended. Cover and simmer for 15 to 20 minutes, until thickened. Stir in the sugar, spices, lime juice, and salt and leave to cool down.

1 Remove the shells from the shrimp, leaving the tails intact. Take out the black vein that runs along the back of each shrimp and leave the shrimp in a cool place while you make the batter and sauce.

PREPARATION: 15 MINUTES + STANDING TIME
COOKING: 20 TO 25 MINUTES
SERVES: 4

2 Make the batter: put the flour, salt, and olive oil in a bowl and make a well in the center. Whisk the egg yolk with the coconut milk, and gradually add to the flour, beating well together. Cover and set aside.

4 Whisk the egg white until stiff and fold gently into the prepared batter. Add the shrimp. Heat the oil for deep-frying to 375°F and fry the shrimp, a few at a time, until golden brown. Remove and then drain on paper towels. Serve immediately with the mango sauce.

SEAFOOD CREOLE
Puerto Rico

1 Make the sofrito (a basic Puerto Rican tomato sauce). Heat the olive oil in a saucepan and add the onion and garlic. Fry over gentle heat until soft and translucent. Add the tomatoes and cilantro, and season with salt and pepper. Simmer over low heat for 20 to 30 minutes, until thickened.

2 In a large skillet, sauté the onions, green bell peppers, and garlic in the olive oil until softened and golden. Stir occasionally and do not allow them to brown.

3 Prepare the seafood, removing any shells from the lobster, shrimp, or crabmeat. Add to the vegetables in the skillet with the prepared sofrito. Simmer gently for 15 minutes.

2 onions, chopped
2 green bell peppers, seeded and chopped
2 garlic cloves, crushed
4 tablespoons olive oil
1 pound mixed seafood, e.g. cooked lobster, large shrimp, crabmeat
4 tablespoons white wine
salt and freshly ground black pepper

For the sofrito:

3 tablespoons olive oil
1 onion, chopped
3 garlic cloves, crushed
1 pound tomatoes, skinned and chopped
1 tablespoon chopped cilantro
salt and freshly ground black pepper

To garnish:

sprigs of cilantro

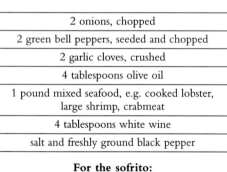

PREPARATION: 30 MINUTES
COOKING: 25 MINUTES
SERVES: 4

4 Add the wine and stir well. Continue cooking for 5 minutes. Adjust the seasoning and serve garnished with cilantro, accompanied by plain boiled rice.

SPICY RED SNAPPER

Jamaica

4 small red snappers
2 teaspoons salt
2 fresh red chiles, seeded and finely chopped
juice of 2 limes
flour for dusting
oil for shallow-frying
1 onion, chopped
1 cup chopped tomato pulp
1¼ cups water
salt and freshly ground black pepper
To serve:
lime wedges
hot pepper sauce

1 Scale and clean the red snappers. Wash well, inside and out, under running cold water and then pat dry with paper towels. Slash the sides of each fish deeply 2 or 3 times, almost through to the bone.

2 Pound the salt and chopped chile together in a mortar and sprinkle over the red snappers. Place the fish in a shallow bowl and pour the lime juice over the top. Cover and leave in a cool place for 1 to 2 hours to marinate.

3 Remove the fish from the bowl, reserving the marinade. Dust them well with flour. Heat the oil in a large skillet and fry the fish until crisp and golden on both sides, turning once during cooking. Remove and drain on paper towels. Keep warm.

PREPARATION: 10 MINUTES +
MARINATING TIME
COOKING: 35 TO 40 MINUTES
SERVES: 4

4 Pour off most of the oil and fry the onion in the oil left in the skillet. When it is soft, add the tomatoes and simmer gently until thickened. Add the water and reserved marinade and bring to the boil. Reduce the heat, add the fried fish and simmer for 5 minutes. Season to taste and serve with lime wedges and hot pepper sauce. Rice makes a good accompaniment.

ROLLED STEAK

Cuba

1 Season one side of the steak with salt and pepper, 1 tablespoon of lime juice, and the garlic. Arrange the ham strips in a layer over the steak. Soak the carrot in the remaining lime juice for 5 minutes. Drain, discarding the lime juice, and arrange the carrot on top of the ham. Sprinkle with sugar and dot with butter.

2 pounds steak
salt and freshly ground black pepper
4 tablespoons lime juice
1 garlic clove, crushed
4 ounces cooked ham, cut into strips
1 carrot, thinly sliced
1 teaspoon sugar
1 tablespoon butter
1 tablespoon red wine vinegar
3 tablespoons dry red wine
3 tablespoons vegetable oil
1 bay leaf
1 onion, thinly sliced
1 green bell pepper, seeded and chopped
1 tablespoon chopped cilantro
1 pound tomatoes, skinned and chopped
1 red bell pepper, seeded and chopped

2 Roll up the steak with the grain. Fasten with wooden toothpicks and tie securely with kitchen string. Mix the vinegar and wine together and pour over the steak. Leave to marinate for 30 minutes.

3 Lift out the steak and pat dry. Reserve the marinade. Heat the oil in a flameproof casserole and brown the steak all over. Add the bay leaf, onion, green bell pepper, cilantro, tomatoes, red bell pepper, and the marinade. Cover and simmer for 2 hours, or until the steak is tender.

4 Lift out the steak and remove the string and toothpicks. Slice into serving portions and then arrange on a warmed serving plate. Pour the sauce over the steak and serve.

PREPARATION: 20 MINUTES +
MARINATING TIME
COOKING: 2 HOURS
SERVES: 4 TO 6

PICADILLO

Minced beef stew (Cuba)

1 Heat the oil in a large, deep skillet and add the onions, garlic, and bell peppers. Fry gently until softened and lightly colored. Add the chile and fry for 1 minute. Stir in the ground beef and cook, stirring constantly, until evenly browned.

2 Add the tomatoes, bay leaf, raisins, olives, cumin, and vinegar. Simmer gently for 20 minutes, until the meat is cooked and the sauce thickens. Stir in the capers and season to taste with salt and pepper. Simmer for 5 more minutes.

3 tablespoons olive oil
2 onions, chopped
3 garlic cloves, crushed
2 green bell peppers, seeded and chopped
1 fresh red chile, seeded and finely chopped
3 cups lean ground beef
4 tomatoes, skinned and chopped
1 bay leaf
½ cup raisins
½ cup stuffed green olives, sliced
½ teaspoon ground cumin
1 tablespoon vinegar
3 tablespoons capers
salt and freshly ground black pepper

For the fried plantains:

3 to 4 ripe black plantains
butter or oil for shallow-frying

PREPARATION: 15 MINUTES
COOKING: 35 MINUTES
SERVES: 4

3 While the picadillo is cooking, prepare and fry the plantains. Cut off the ends and peel the plantains. Cut each one in half lengthwise and then cut each piece in half again crosswise.

4 Heat the butter or oil in a heavy skillet and add the plantains. Fry gently until they are golden brown on both sides, turning them once. Drain on paper towels and serve immediately with the picadillo.

BEEF AND PINEAPPLE KEBOBS

Anguilla

| 1 pound beef steak |
| 3 tomatoes |
| 2 onions |
| 1 green bell pepper |
| 12 pineapple cubes, fresh or canned |
| **For the marinade:** |
| 1 tablespoon molasses |
| 4 tablespoons pineapple juice |
| 2 tablespoons vinegar |
| 1 tablespoon oil |
| salt and freshly ground black pepper |

1 Make the marinade: put the molasses, pineapple juice, vinegar, and oil in a bowl and mix well together. Add a little salt and some freshly ground black pepper.

3 Cut the tomatoes into quarters. Peel the onions and cut them into small chunks. Remove the ribs and seeds from the green bell pepper, and cut it into squares.

4 Thread the steak, tomatoes, onions, bell pepper, and pineapple chunks alternately on to 4 long or 8 short skewers. Brush them with the reserved marinade. Cook under a hot broiler for about 10 minutes, turning frequently and basting often. Serve with plain boiled rice with the remaining marinade poured over the top.

2 Cut the steak into 1-inch cubes and add to the marinade. Cover and leave in a cool place for at least 1 hour. Remove the steak and reserve the marinade for basting the kebobs.

PREPARATION: 20 MINUTES +
MARINATING TIME
COOKING: 10 MINUTES
SERVES: 4

COLOMBO DE PORC

Pork curry (Martinique)

3 tablespoons peanut oil

2 tablespoons butter

2 pounds lean pork loin, cubed

2 onions, finely chopped

2 garlic cloves, crushed

few sprigs of fresh thyme

few sprigs of parsley, chopped

$5/8$ cup water or broth

1 tablespoon white wine vinegar

1 chayote, peeled and cubed

1 eggplant, peeled and cubed

2 tomatoes, skinned, seeded, and chopped

For the Poudre de Colombo:

pinch of turmeric

1 teaspoon ground coriander

2 garlic cloves, crushed

2 fresh red chiles, seeded and finely chopped

2 teaspoons mustard seeds

4 allspice berries

freshly ground black pepper

2 Heat the oil and butter in a deep skillet or saucepan and add the pork, onions, and garlic. Fry over medium heat, stirring frequently, until the pork is browned on all sides and the onions are softened.

4 Add the herbs, water or broth, and the vinegar. Cover the pan and cook gently for about 30 minutes. Add the remaining ingredients and continue cooking, uncovered, for about 15 minutes, or until the vegetables are tender and the sauce reduced and thickened. Serve with rice.

1 Make the Poudre de Colombo: put the turmeric, coriander, garlic, chiles, mustard seeds, allspice berries, and black pepper in a mortar. Mash with a pestle to make a paste.

3 Add the Poudre de Colombo paste to the pork and onions in the pan and stir well. Cook over gentle heat for about 3 minutes, stirring occasionally.

PREPARATION:
15 MINUTES
COOKING: 1 HOUR
SERVES 4

SPICED PORK ROAST

Jamaica

1 (4-pound) pork loin
½ cup dark rum
2½ cups meat broth
2 teaspoons arrowroot (or cornstarch)

For the seasoning:
½ teaspoon ground cloves
½ teaspoon ground allspice
1 teaspoon ground ginger
2 garlic cloves, crushed
1 bay leaf, crumbled
salt and freshly ground black pepper

For the basting sauce:
6 tablespoons soft brown sugar
juice of 1 lime
3 tablespoons rum

1 Mix all the seasoning ingredients together in a small bowl. With a sharp knife, cut through the fat on the pork loin in a diamond pattern. Rub the seasoning over the scored fat.

2 Place the pork loin in a roasting pan. Pour the rum and ½ cup of the broth over the pork. Place in a preheated oven at 350°F and roast for 1¾ to 2 hours.

3 Mix together the ingredients for the basting sauce and blend well. After 1 hour, remove the pork from the oven and baste with the sauce. Return to the oven for the remainder of the cooking time, adding more stock or a little water if necessary to moisten the meat.

4 When the meat is cooked, transfer it to a serving plate and keep warm. Drain off some of the fat and add the remaining basting sauce and meat broth. Stir well to scrape up any pork residues in the pan. Place over heat and bring to the boil, stirring. Mix the arrowroot with 1 tablespoon of water and stir into the broth until thickened. Serve with the roast pork.

PREPARATION: 10 MINUTES
COOKING: 2 HOURS
SERVES: 6

CHICKEN PILAU

Trinidad

1 Put the seasoning ingredients in a mortar and pound well with a pestle until the garlic and allspice berries are crushed and blended with the salt, pepper, and herbs. Rub this mixture all over the chicken pieces and leave in a cool place or the refrigerator for several hours (overnight if wished).

3 Add the onion, garlic, red bell pepper and chile, and fry over gentle heat until softened but not browned. Add the rice to the skillet and turn in the oil until all the grains are glistening. Stir in the tomatoes, chicken broth, strands of saffron, and thyme.

2 Heat the oil and butter in a large, deep skillet and add the seasoned chicken pieces. Fry over moderate heat, turning several times, until they are golden brown all over. Remove from the pan and keep warm.

PREPARATION: 10 MINUTES +
MARINATING TIME
COOKING: 40 MINUTES
SERVES: 6

1 (4-pound) chicken, cut into pieces
3 tablespoons peanut oil
1 tablespoon butter
1 onion, finely chopped
2 garlic cloves, crushed
1 red bell pepper, seeded and chopped
1 red chile, seeded and finely chopped
1½ cups long-grain rice
2 tomatoes, skinned and chopped
3¾ cups chicken broth
few strands of saffron
sprig of thyme
For the seasoning:
salt and freshly ground black pepper
1 teaspoon dried mixed herbs
2 allspice berries
1 garlic clove, peeled
To garnish:
½ cup roasted peanuts
chopped fresh red chile

4 Return the chicken pieces to the skillet, cover and simmer for about 20 minutes, or until the rice is tender, the liquid is absorbed, and the chicken is cooked. Keep checking and stirring the rice to prevent it sticking. Add more liquid if necessary. Serve hot sprinkled with peanuts and chile.

CHICKEN IN COCONUT MILK

Martinique

3 Return the chicken to the skillet and pour in the coconut milk. Sprinkle with saffron and season with salt and pepper. Stir well and simmer for 30 to 40 minutes, until the chicken is cooked and tender, and the sauce has reduced. Sprinkle with parsley.

1 Heat the peanut oil in a large, deep skillet and add the chicken quarters. Fry gently over moderate heat until the chicken is golden brown all over. Turn the chicken occasionally in the oil.

| 3 tablespoons peanut oil |
| 4 chicken quarters |
| 2 onions, finely chopped |
| 2 garlic cloves, crushed |
| 1 fresh red chile, finely chopped |
| $1^7/_8$ cups coconut milk |
| few strands of saffron |
| salt and pepper |
| **For the rice:** |
| $1^1/_2$ cups long-grain rice |
| 5 cups water |
| salt |
| **To garnish:** |
| 2 tablespoons chopped parsley |

2 Remove the chicken and set aside. Add the onions, garlic, and chile to the skillet and fry gently for about 5 minutes, until soft. Do not allow the onions to brown—they should be only lightly colored.

PREPARATION: 10 MINUTES
COOKING: 45 TO 50 MINUTES
SERVES: 4

4 Meanwhile, prepare the rice. Wash it thoroughly and drain well. Bring the salted water to the boil and quickly tip in the rice. Simmer vigorously for 15 minutes. Drain and rinse, and then return to the saucepan. Cover and simmer, without water, for 15 to 20 minutes, until the rice is dry and cooked. Serve with the chicken.

CHICKEN WITH PINEAPPLE

Cuba

1 (4-pound) chicken, cut into 6 pieces
juice of 1 lime
grated zest of 1 lime
salt and freshly ground black pepper
flour for dusting
2 tablespoons olive oil
1 tablespoon butter
1 onion, chopped
1 garlic clove, crushed
1 fresh red chile, seeded and finely chopped
2 tomatoes, skinned and chopped
3 tablespoons raisins
1 teaspoon brown sugar
For the sauce:
1 ripe pineapple, peeled and cored
2 tablespoons rum

3 Add the onion, garlic, and chile, and fry gently for 5 minutes. Add the tomatoes, raisins, and brown sugar, mix well and cook gently for a further 10 minutes.

1 Put the chicken pieces in a large bowl. Rub them all over with the lime juice and grated zest, and sprinkle with salt and pepper. Set aside for 30 minutes for the chicken to absorb the flavor of the lime.

PREPARATION: 15 MINUTES +
MARINATING TIME
COOKING: 30 MINUTES
SERVES: 6

2 Dust the chicken pieces lightly with flour. Heat the oil and butter in a large, heavy skillet. Add the chicken to the hot oil and fry gently over low heat until it is tender and golden brown. Turn the chicken frequently to cook it on both sides.

4 Meanwhile, chop and crush the pineapple, and then mix to a pulp with all its juice in an electric blender. Transfer to a pan and simmer gently until reduced to a quarter of its original volume. Stir in the rum, and then pour the sauce over the chicken and serve.

CHICKEN CALYPSO

Dominica

5 tablespoons peanut oil

1 (4-pound) chicken, cut into pieces

2 cups long-grain rice

1 onion, finely chopped

1 green bell pepper, seeded and finely chopped

$^1/_2$ teaspoon saffron strands

$2^1/_2$ cups chicken broth

2-inch piece of lime peel

1 tablespoon rum

dash of Angostura bitters

salt and freshly ground black pepper

$1^1/_4$ cups sliced mushrooms

1 Heat 3 tablespoons of the oil in a large, heavy skillet and add the chicken pieces. Fry them until they are golden brown all over, turning them occasionally. Remove the chicken and keep warm.

2 Add the rice, onion, and green bell pepper to the skillet, and stir well. Fry gently until golden and the rice grains are translucent. Stir in the saffron, chicken broth, lime peel, rum, and Angostura bitters.

3 Transfer the rice and vegetable mixture to a heavy flameproof casserole dish, and place the chicken pieces on top. Season well with salt and freshly ground black pepper.

4 Fry the mushrooms in the remaining oil in a clean skillet for 5 minutes. Add to the casserole and then cover and simmer gently for about 30 minutes, until the chicken is cooked and all the liquid absorbed. Remove the lid for the last 5 minutes so that the rice is light and fluffy. Serve hot.

PREPARATION: 10 MINUTES
COOKING: 50 MINUTES
SERVES: 4 TO 6

JAMAICAN JERKED CHICKEN

Jamaica

1 ounce allspice berries

2-inch cinnamon stick

1 teaspoon freshly grated nutmeg

1 fresh red chile, seeded and finely chopped

4 scallions, thinly sliced

1 bay leaf, crumbled

salt and freshly ground black pepper

1 tablespoon dark rum

6 chicken pieces

For the pineapple chutney:

2 fresh pineapples, peeled and chopped

1-inch piece fresh gingerroot, peeled and finely chopped

1 onion, finely chopped

1 fresh red chile, seeded and finely chopped

½ cup vinegar

1 cup dark brown sugar

1 Make the jerked seasoning: pound the allspice berries, cinnamon, and nutmeg in a mortar, or grind them to a powder in an electric grinder. Add the chile, scallions, bay leaf, and seasoning to the mortar and continue pounding to a thick paste.

2 Stir the rum into the paste and mix well. Slash the chicken deeply on the skin side 2 or 3 times, and then rub the jerked seasoning paste all over the chicken. Cover and leave in the refrigerator for 1 to 2 hours.

3 Meanwhile, make the pineapple chutney. Put all the ingredients in a saucepan and stir well. Place over moderate heat and stir until the sugar has completely dissolved. Bring to the boil and then reduce the heat a little. Cook vigorously, stirring occasionally, until the chutney thickens.

4 Pour the chutney into sterilized glass jars and seal. If wished, it can be made in advance and kept for 2 to 3 weeks in a refrigerator. Roast the jerked chicken at 400°F for 20 to 30 minutes, or cook under a hot broiler. Serve with the pineapple chutney and plain boiled rice.

PREPARATION: 20 MINUTES + MARINATING TIME
COOKING: 20 TO 30 MINUTES
SERVES: 6

BROILED CHICKEN CREOLE
St Lucia

1 Prepare the seasoning: put the scallions, onion, garlic, chile, herbs, and allspice berries in a bowl. Add the lime juice and olive oil and stir well to mix thoroughly together.

6 chicken breasts, skinned and boned
salt and freshly ground black pepper

For the seasoning:
2 scallions, finely chopped
1/2 red onion, finely chopped
2 garlic cloves, crushed
1 fresh red chile, seeded and finely chopped
3 chives, chopped
few sprigs of thyme, chopped
few sprigs of parsley, chopped
3 allspice berries, crushed
juice of 1 lime
2 tablespoons olive oil

For the avocado sauce:
1 large ripe avocado
1 tablespoon finely chopped onion
1/2 garlic clove, crushed
cayenne pepper, to taste
lime juice (optional)

2 Slash the chicken breasts 2 or 3 times on both sides, and season lightly with salt and pepper. Rub the seasoning over both sides of each chicken breast, pressing it into the slashes. Chill in the refrigerator for 2 to 3 hours.

3 Put the chicken breasts on a rack in a broiler pan and cook under a hot broiler, turning once, until cooked on both sides. Take care that the herbs do not burn. Alternatively, cook in a preheated oven at 400°F for about 20 minutes.

4 While the chicken is cooking, make the avocado sauce. Mash the avocado to a smooth paste and beat in the onion, garlic, and a little cayenne pepper. Add a little lime juice, if wished. This will prevent the sauce discoloring. Serve with the broiled chicken, with some plain boiled rice.

PREPARATION: 10 MINUTES +
MARINATING TIME
COOKING: 15 TO 20 MINUTES
SERVES: 4

CHICKEN CURRY

Guadeloupe

1 Heat the oil in a heavy skillet and add the chicken pieces. Fry over moderate heat until golden brown all over, turning several times to cook both sides. Remove from the skillet and place in a flameproof casserole dish.

2 Add the onions, garlic, and chile to the skillet and cook, stirring occasionally, over medium heat until the onions are softened and golden, about 5 minutes.

3 Add the curry powder to the onion mixture and stir well. Continue cooking for 3 minutes, stirring. Add the eggplant, chayote, papaya, and tomatoes, and cook for 2 to 3 minutes.

5 tablespoons peanut oil
1 (4-pound) chicken, cut into 6 or 8 serving pieces
2 onions, finely chopped
1 garlic clove, crushed
1 fresh red chile, seeded and finely chopped
2 tablespoons curry powder
8 ounces peeled and cubed eggplant
1 chayote, peeled and cubed
1 unripe green papaya, peeled and sliced
2 tomatoes, skinned and chopped
⁵/₈ cup chicken broth
⁵/₈ cup coconut milk
2 tablespoons lime juice
salt and freshly ground black pepper
1 tablespoon rum

4 Put the curried mixture into the casserole with the chicken and add the chicken broth and coconut milk. Cover and simmer for about 30 minutes, until the chicken is cooked and the vegetables are tender. Stir in the lime juice, seasoning, and rum. Serve with plain boiled rice and fried bananas.

PREPARATION: 10 MINUTES
COOKING: 50 MINUTES
SERVES: 4 TO 6

COO-COO

Barbados

1 Wash the okra and cut off the stems. Cut them into ¼-inch thick slices. Bring the water to the boil in a large saucepan and add the prepared okra and the salt. Boil until tender.

2 Slowly add the cornmeal to the saucepan in a thin stream, stirring all the time with a wooden spoon. Keep stirring to prevent any lumps forming and removing any cornmeal from the sides of the pan.

3 Add the sugar and continue cooking over moderate heat for about 5 to 10 minutes, stirring all the time. When cooked, the coo-coo mixture will be thick and smooth.

| 12 okra |
| 5 cups water |
| good pinch of salt |
| 1 ⅓ cups yellow cornmeal |
| 1 tablespoon sugar |
| 2 tablespoons butter |

To serve:

| cooked sweet potatoes |
| sliced tomatoes |
| sliced pimentos |

4 Place the butter in a warmed round bowl or basin and add the coo-coo. Roll it around in the bowl until it forms a ball. Serve, cut into slices, with sweet potatoes, tomatoes, and pimentos.

PREPARATION: 10 MINUTES
COOKING: 20 TO 25 MINUTES
SERVES: 6

PUMPKIN CURRY

St Lucia

1 Put the grated fresh coconut in a bowl and add the coconut water. You can drain this out of a fresh coconut by piercing it a couple of times with a skewer and draining out the liquid. Leave the coconut to soak for about 30 minutes.

4 Add the pumpkin, tomatoes, coconut, and coconut water. Bring to the boil and then reduce the heat to a bare simmer. Cover the pan and cook gently for 15 to 20 minutes, until the pumpkin is tender but not mushy. Season to taste with salt and pepper and serve hot.

2 Heat the vegetable oil in a large, heavy saucepan and add the onion, green bell pepper, and garlic. Fry gently over very low heat, stirring occasionally, until the onion and bell pepper are softened and golden brown.

3 Add the fresh gingerroot, turmeric, chiles, and cloves to the onion and bell pepper mixture. Stir well and continue cooking over low heat for 2 to 3 minutes, stirring.

| 4 ounces fresh coconut, shredded |
| 1¼ cups coconut water (from a fresh coconut) |
| 2 tablespoons vegetable oil |
| 1 onion, chopped |
| 1 green bell pepper, seeded and chopped |
| 4 garlic cloves, crushed |
| 2 slices fresh gingerroot, peeled and finely chopped |
| 1 tablespoon turmeric |
| 2 fresh green chiles, seeded and finely chopped |
| ¼ teaspoon ground cloves |
| 1½ pounds pumpkin, peeled, seeded, and cut into 1-inch cubes |
| 2 tomatoes, skinned and chopped |
| salt and freshly ground black pepper |

PREPARATION: 20 MINUTES +
SOAKING TIME
COOKING: 30 TO 35 MINUTES
SERVES: 4 TO 6

CHAYOTE AU GRATIN

Guadeloupe

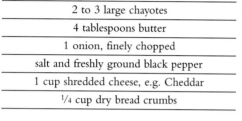

| 2 to 3 large chayotes |
| 4 tablespoons butter |
| 1 onion, finely chopped |
| salt and freshly ground black pepper |
| 1 cup shredded cheese, e.g. Cheddar |
| ¼ cup dry bread crumbs |

1 Put the chayotes into a large saucepan of lightly salted water and bring to the boil. Parboil for 20 to 30 minutes, or until the chayotes are slightly soft. Remove and cool.

3 Heat the butter in a small skillet and add the onion. Cook until soft and transparent. Season to taste with salt and pepper and stir in the chayote pulp. Cook gently over low heat for 2 minutes. Stir in half of the shredded cheese.

4 Pile the chayote and onion mixture into the reserved shells and top with the remaining cheese and bread crumbs. Place on a cookie sheet and cook in a preheated oven at 350°F for 15 to 20 minutes, until delicately browned.

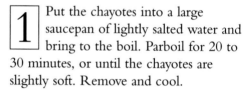

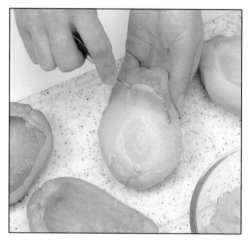

2 Cut each chayote in half lengthwise and carefully scoop out the pulp, leaving the shells intact. Chop and mash the pulp, and reserve the shells.

PREPARATION: 10 MINUTES
COOKING: 35 TO 50 MINUTES
SERVES: 4 TO 6

FRIJOLES NEGROS

Black beans (Cuba)

1 Wash the black beans thoroughly under running cold water and then drain them. Put them in a large, heavy saucepan with the water and bring to the boil.

2 Reduce the heat to a bare simmer, cover the saucepan, and cook very gently for about 1½ to 2 hours, until the beans are tender but not mushy. Keep checking the beans and adding more liquid if necessary.

PREPARATION: 15 MINUTES
COOKING: 2 TO 2½ HOURS
SERVES: 6

3 While the beans are cooking, heat the oil in a skillet and add the salt pork or ham. Sauté gently for 2 to 3 minutes and then add the onion, garlic, green bell pepper, and chile. Cook, stirring occasionally, until the vegetables are softened.

4 Add the onion mixture to the pan of beans, together with the bay leaf and a little salt and pepper. Simmer gently for 30 minutes. Remove a spoonful of beans and mash well. Return to the pan and stir. The consistency of the sauce should be thick but not too liquid. Serve hot, garnished with chopped scallions.

2 ½ cups dried black beans
3 cups water
2 tablespoons vegetable oil
2 ounces salt pork or ham, chopped
1 onion, finely chopped
1 garlic clove, crushed
1 green bell pepper, seeded and chopped
1 fresh green chile, seeded and finely chopped
1 bay leaf
salt and freshly ground black pepper
To garnish:
2 scallions, chopped

OKRA CREOLE-STYLE

St Lucia

1 Prepare the okra: wash it well and then pat dry with paper towels. Cut off the stems with a sharp knife and slice the okra into ¼-inch rounds. Set aside.

3 Add the tomatoes and fresh corn kernels and stir well. Season with salt and pepper to taste, and then add the lime juice. Reduce the heat and cook gently over low heat for 15 to 20 minutes, until the okra are tender and the sauce is reduced and thickened.

12 to 16 okra
3 tablespoons peanut oil
1 large onion, thinly sliced
1 green bell pepper, seeded and chopped
2 garlic cloves, crushed
1 pound tomatoes, skinned and chopped
1½ cups fresh corn kernels
salt and freshly ground black pepper
juice of ½ lime
dash of hot pepper sauce
To garnish:
fresh cilantro

2 Heat the peanut oil in a large, heavy skillet and add the onion, green bell pepper, and garlic. Fry gently over medium heat until slightly browned, stirring occasionally. Add the okra and continue cooking for 5 minutes.

4 While the okra are cooking, stir occasionally to stop the sauce sticking to the base of the skillet. Just before serving, add a dash of hot pepper sauce. Transfer to a serving dish and garnish with cilantro.

PREPARATION: 10 MINUTES
COOKING: 25 TO 30 MINUTES
SERVES: 4 TO 6

BANANA CURRY

Bermuda

1 Melt the butter in a large, heavy saucepan. Add the onions and fry gently over very low heat until softened and translucent. Take care that they do not brown.

2 Meanwhile, soak the golden raisins in a little boiling water for 2 to 3 minutes to plump them up. Drain and add to the onions with the apple and salt. Stir in the flour and curry powder and cook, stirring, for 3 to 4 minutes.

3 Remove the saucepan from the heat and gradually stir in the coconut milk and water, a little at a time. Return to the heat and cook very gently, stirring until thickened.

4 tablespoons butter
2 small onions, chopped
½ cup golden raisins
1 apple, peeled, cored, and diced
½ teaspoon salt
4 tablespoons flour
2 teaspoons curry powder
1¼ cups coconut milk
1¼ cups water
4 under-ripe green bananas, peeled and diagonally sliced
4 hard-boiled eggs, quartered

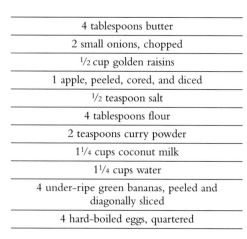

4 Add the bananas and continue cooking gently over low heat for about 7 minutes. Add the eggs to the curry and heat through. Serve with mango chutney and plain boiled rice.

PREPARATION: 10 MINUTES
COOKING: 20 TO 25 MINUTES
SERVES: 4

ORANGE-BAKED SWEET POTATOES

Bahamas

5 sweet potatoes

5 large oranges

4 tablespoons cream

2 tablespoons butter

1 tablespoon sugar

1 tablespoon dark rum

salt and freshly grated black pepper

pinch of ground cinnamon

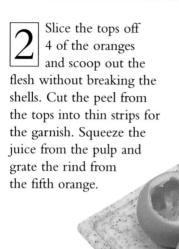

2 Slice the tops off 4 of the oranges and scoop out the flesh without breaking the shells. Cut the peel from the tops into thin strips for the garnish. Squeeze the juice from the pulp and grate the rind from the fifth orange.

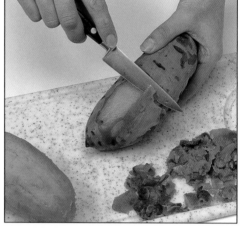

1 Wash the sweet potatoes and place in a saucepan of lightly salted water. Bring to the boil and then continue boiling for about 30 minutes, until the sweet potatoes are tender. Drain and peel them, and then set aside.

3 Put the peeled sweet potatoes in a bowl and mash thoroughly. Add the cream, butter, sugar, and rum and mix well together, beating until blended. Add 4 tablespoons of the squeezed orange juice and the grated rind. Season with salt and pepper and the cinnamon.

4 Spoon the mashed potato mixture into the 4 orange shells. Place on a cookie sheet and then bake in a preheated oven at 350°F for 15 to 20 minutes, until golden brown on top. Garnish with the reserved strips of orange peel and serve.

PREPARATION: 10 MINUTES

COOKING: 50 MINUTES

SERVES: 4

RICE AND PEAS

Jamaica

1 Put the dried red kidney beans in a large bowl and cover with cold water. Leave to soak overnight. The following day, rinse the kidney beans and drain well.

2 Put the kidney beans in a large saucepan and add 3³/₄ cups boiling water. Cook the beans over moderate heat for about 30 minutes, or until they are almost tender.

3 Add the coconut milk, thyme, scallions, and chile to the saucepan. Season with salt and pepper and bring back to boiling point. Boil rapidly for 5 minutes.

4 Add the rice and stir well. Cover and simmer gently over very low heat until the rice is tender and all the liquid has been absorbed. This will take about 20 to 25 minutes. If there is any remaining liquid, drain the rice and "peas" (kidney beans). Transfer to a serving dish and serve hot.

1 cup dried red kidney beans
2¹/₂ cups coconut milk
2 sprigs of fresh thyme
2 scallions, finely chopped
1 fresh green chile, seeded and finely chopped
salt and freshly ground black pepper
2 cups long-grain rice

PREPARATION: 5 MINUTES +
SOAKING TIME
COOKING: 55 MINUTES
SERVES: 6

STUFFED BELL PEPPERS

Trinidad

1 Place the bell peppers in a large saucepan and cover with cold water. Bring to the boil, then reduce the heat and simmer gently until the bell peppers are tender but still firm. Drain and allow to cool.

2 Prepare the stuffing: heat the oil in a large skillet and add the onion, garlic, and chile. Fry gently over low heat until the onion is softened and golden brown.

3 Add the ground beef and stir well. Continue cooking over low heat until well browned. Add the lemon rind and cooked rice. Season with salt and pepper and paprika. Cook gently for 5 minutes and then stir in the chives.

4 large green bell peppers

2 tablespoons vegetable oil

1 small onion, finely chopped

1 garlic clove, crushed

1 fresh red chile, seeded and finely chopped

½ cup ground beef

grated rind of 1 lemon

4 tablespoons cooked rice

salt and freshly ground black pepper

pinch of paprika

few chives, chopped

4 tomatoes, thinly sliced

To garnish:

chopped chives

PREPARATION: 15 MINUTES
COOKING: 45 MINUTES
SERVES: 4

4 Slice the tops off the bell peppers and scoop out the seeds. Fill with the stuffing and stand in a baking pan. Surround with the tomatoes and bake in a preheated oven at 350°F for about 20 minutes. Serve sprinkled with chives.

RUM CREPES

Barbados

1 Sift the flour into a bowl and make a well in the center. Stir in the sugar, eggs, olive oil, and rum. Blend thoroughly, drawing in the flour from the sides, until the mixture is smooth.

2 Gradually add the milk, a little at a time, beating well between each addition. The batter should be smooth with the consistency of light cream. Add a little more milk if necessary and then let stand for 1 hour.

3 Brush a small skillet with a little oil and heat thoroughly. Pour in sufficient batter to cover the base of the skillet thinly, tilting the skillet until evenly covered. Cook until the underside of the batter is set and golden brown, and then flip the crepe over and cook the other side. Remove and keep warm. Cook the remaining crepes in the same way.

4 Make the filling: beat the cream until thick and gently stir in the rum and sugar. Spread the warm crepes with the filling and roll up or fold over. Sprinkle with shaved chocolate and serve the crepes immediately.

1 cup flour	
1 teaspoon sugar	
2 eggs	
1 tablespoon olive oil	
1 tablespoon rum	
$1\frac{1}{4}$ cups milk	
oil for frying	
For the filling:	
$1\frac{1}{4}$ cups heavy cream	
2 tablespoons rum	
2 teaspoons sugar	
To decorate:	
chocolate shavings	

PREPARATION: 10 MINUTES +
STANDING TIME
COOKING: 10 MINUTES
SERVES: 4 TO 6

STUFFED BANANAS

Haiti

1 Put the raisins in a small bowl with 2 tablespoons of the rum and set aside while you prepare the dessert. The raisins plump up in the rum and are used for decoration.

2 Peel the bananas and then cut each one in half lengthwise, and then in half crosswise. Place them in a bowl and sprinkle with the lime juice to prevent discoloration. Set aside.

3 In a bowl, beat the butter and sugar together until the mixture is smooth and creamy. Add the remaining rum, and beat thoroughly. Fold the cashews into the butter mixture.

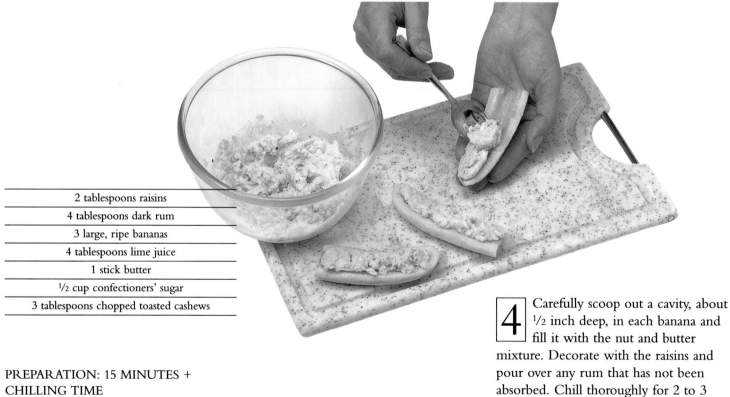

| 2 tablespoons raisins |
| 4 tablespoons dark rum |
| 3 large, ripe bananas |
| 4 tablespoons lime juice |
| 1 stick butter |
| ½ cup confectioners' sugar |
| 3 tablespoons chopped toasted cashews |

4 Carefully scoop out a cavity, about ½ inch deep, in each banana and fill it with the nut and butter mixture. Decorate with the raisins and pour over any rum that has not been absorbed. Chill thoroughly for 2 to 3 hours before serving.

PREPARATION: 15 MINUTES +
CHILLING TIME
SERVES: 3 TO 6

CLAFOUTIS AUX FRUITS EXOTIQUES

Exotic fruit batter dessert (Guadeloupe)

1 Cut the fresh pineapple and mango flesh into ½-inch chunks. Put the prepared fruit in a bowl and sprinkle with the rum. Set aside while you make the batter.

2 Break the eggs into a bowl and beat lightly together. Sift the flour and salt and blend well with the beaten eggs. Beat in the sugar until the batter is smooth.

PREPARATION: 15 MINUTES
COOKING: 25 TO 30 MINUTES
SERVES: 4 TO 6

4 Arrange the pineapple and mango in a buttered shallow, ovenproof dish. Pour the batter mixture over them and bake in a preheated oven at 400°F for 25 to 30 minutes, until risen and set. Cool a little and then serve sprinkled with sugar.

3 Heat the milk with the vanilla bean but do not allow to boil. Remove from the heat and allow to infuse for 5 minutes. Remove the vanilla bean and strain the milk into the egg batter, a little at a time, beating well until thoroughly blended. Beat in the rum from the soaked fruit.

1 pound fresh pineapple and mango, peeled
2 tablespoons dark rum
3 eggs
2 tablespoons flour
pinch of salt
¼ cup sugar
1¼ cups milk
1 vanilla bean
butter for greasing
sugar for sprinkling

BANANA LOAF

St Lucia

1 Put the butter and sugar in a large mixing bowl and beat together until light and creamy. Beat in the eggs, one at a time, and then stir in the rum (if using).

2 Sift all the dry ingredients—the self rising flour, salt, baking soda, grated nutmeg, and ground cinnamon—into another clean bowl and set aside.

PREPARATION: 15 MINUTES
COOKING: 1 HOUR
MAKES: 1 LOAF

3 Peel the bananas and, using a fork, mash them with the vanilla extract. Gradually add the flour mixture and the banana mixture to the egg, butter, and sugar mixture, beating thoroughly after each addition. Toss the raisins and walnuts in a little flour and then stir into the banana mixture.

1 stick butter, softened
$^3/_4$ cup sugar
2 eggs
2 tablespoons rum (optional)
2$^1/_4$ cups self rising flour
$^1/_2$ teaspoon salt
$^1/_4$ teaspoon baking soda
1 teaspoon grated nutmeg
$^1/_2$ teaspoon ground cinnamon
2 to 3 large, ripe bananas
1 teaspoon vanilla extract
$^1/_2$ cup raisins
$^3/_4$ cup chopped walnuts

4 Pour the mixture into a greased 9 x 5-inch loaf pan. Bake in a preheated oven at 350°F for 1 hour, or until a skewer inserted into the center of the bread comes out clean. Turn out and cool on a wire rack. Serve sliced, with or without butter. In the Caribbean, this is served as a dessert or may be offered for breakfast.

LIME MERINGUE PIE

Virgin Islands

1 Make the pie filling: put the grated lime rind and juice in a heavy-based saucepan with the sugar and eggs. Place over very low heat and stir well.

2 Cut the butter into small dice and add to the lime mixture in the pan, one cube at a time. Continue stirring all the time over low heat, until all the butter has been incorporated and the mixture is hot.

3 Pour the lime mixture into the prepared pie crust and place in the center of a preheated oven at 375°F for about 10 minutes, or until the filling is just set. Remove from the oven and cool.

1 (9-inch) baked pie shell
For the filling:
grated rind and juice of 3 limes
$3/4$ cup sugar
3 eggs, beaten
2 sticks butter
For the meringue:
3 egg whites
6 tablespoons sugar

4 Make the meringue topping: beat the egg whites until they stand in stiff peaks. Gradually beat in the sugar, a little at a time. Pile the meringue on top of the lime filling and bake in a preheated oven at 375°F for 12 to 15 minutes, until the meringue is delicately browned. Serve hot or cold.

PREPARATION: 15 MINUTES
COOKING: 35 MINUTES
SERVES: 6 TO 8

BANANA RUM FRITTERS

Martinique

4 large, ripe bananas	
2 tablespoons sugar	
5 tablespoons dark rum	
oil for deep-frying	
For the batter:	
$^3/_4$ cup flour	
pinch of salt	
1 tablespoon olive oil	
$^5/_8$ cup water	
2 egg whites	
To serve:	
vanilla sugar	
ground cinnamon	

1 Peel the bananas and then cut them diagonally into slices, about $^1/_2$-inch thick. Place them in a shallow dish and sprinkle with sugar. Pour the rum over the top and set aside for $1^1/_2$ hours, turning from time to time.

2 Meanwhile, make the batter: sift the flour and salt together into a bowl. Make a well in the center and gradually mix in the oil and water. Mix to a smooth batter and let stand for 1 hour.

3 Just before the batter is needed, beat the egg whites stiffly and then lightly fold them into the batter. Drain the banana slices and dip them into the batter so that they are completely coated.

PREPARATION: 15 MINUTES + STANDING TIME
COOKING: 10 MINUTES
SERVES: 4

4 Heat the oil for deep-frying and when it is very hot (375°F), fry the banana pieces, a few at a time, until golden brown on both sides. Drain on paper towels. Serve the fritters really hot, sprinkled with vanilla sugar and cinnamon.

AVOCADO ICE CREAM

Jamaica

1 Break the eggs into a large mixing bowl and beat lightly together. Add ¹/₄ cup of the sugar and beat lightly. Heat the milk in a saucepan until very hot but do not allow it to boil.

2 Pour the hot milk into the egg mixture, stirring well to mix thoroughly. Place the bowl over a pan of hot simmering water and stir until the custard thickens and coats the back of a spoon. Alternatively, pour into the top of a double boiler and stir until the custard is thick. Stir in the vanilla or almond extract and then remove from the heat and set aside to cool.

3 Cut the avocados in half and remove the peel and seeds. Mash them in a bowl with the remaining sugar and lime juice. Beat well.

4 eggs
¹/₂ cup sugar
2¹/₂ cups milk
¹/₂ teaspoon vanilla or almond extract
2 medium-sized ripe avocado pears
good squeeze of lime juice

PREPARATION: 20 MINUTES +
FREEZING TIME
SERVES: 6-8

4 Mix the custard into the mashed avocado and turn into a freezer container. Freeze lightly until the mixture is slushy. Remove from the refrigerator, beat again and then return to the freezer until frozen.

106

MANGO FOOL

Jamaica

1 Peel the mangoes and cut out the pits. Chop the flesh into small pieces and place in a saucepan with the sugar, lime juice, and water. Simmer gently over low heat until soft and pulpy.

2 Push the mango mixture through a sieve, and then beat the purée thoroughly until smooth. Cover and set aside to cool while you make the custard mixture.

PREPARATION: 15 MINUTES +
CHILLING TIME
COOKING: 15 TO 20 MINUTES
SERVES: 4 TO 6

3 Break the egg into a bowl and beat lightly. Heat the milk without boiling and then stir into the beaten egg. Return to the heat and stir constantly over very low heat until the custard thickens. Do not allow to boil.

4 Remove the custard from the heat and allow to cool. Stir in the mango purée and the cream. Do not blend thoroughly; the fool should look streaky. Pour into glasses or individual dishes and chill before serving.

6 mangoes
$1/2$ cup sugar
juice of $1/2$ lime
$5/8$ cup water
1 egg
$5/8$ cup milk
$1/2$ cup heavy cream

SAUCES, DRINKS AND CHUTNEYS

RUM PUNCH

1 part fresh lime juice
2 parts sugar
3 parts dark rum
4 parts crushed ice
dash of Angostura bitters
grated nutmeg
To decorate:
sprig of mint or lime leaf
sliced pineapple or orange

Put the lime juice, sugar, rum, ice, and bitters in a cocktail shaker, and shake together vigorously. Pour into a glass and serve with grated nutmeg, decorated with a sprig of mint or a lime leaf, and fresh pineapple or orange slices.

WEST INDIES CHUTNEY

2 pounds green apples, peeled, cored, and chopped
1 large onion, finely chopped
1/2 cup soft brown sugar
1 teaspoon salt
1/2 tablespoon mixed pickling spice
1/2 teaspoon ground ginger
1 1/4 cups vinegar
1/2 cup molasses

Put all the ingredients in a large, heavy pan and stir thoroughly. Bring to the boil, stirring all the time. Reduce the heat and simmer, uncovered, for 2 hours, until the chutney is thick. Allow to cool a little before bottling in sterilized jars. Store in a cool, dark place. Serve with grilled or broiled meat, chicken, and curries. Makes 2 to 3 jars

BARBECUE SAUCE

2 large onions, chopped
4 garlic cloves, crushed
2 tablespoons tomato paste
2 teaspoons cayenne pepper
4 tablespoons lime juice
4 tablespoons olive oil
2 celery sticks, chopped
2 tablespoons brown sugar
2 sprigs of thyme
4 chiles, chopped
1 tablespoon salt
4 bay leaves

Mix the onion, garlic, tomato paste, cayenne pepper, and lime juice. Heat the oil in a saucepan and add the onion mixture. Cook very gently for 10 minutes, and then add the remaining ingredients. Bring to the boil and then simmer gently for 30 minutes. Serve with broiled meat, chicken, or fish. Serves 4 to 6

CREOLE PEPPER SAUCE

1 onion, finely chopped
1 green bell pepper, seeded and chopped
1 red bell pepper, seeded and chopped
2 garlic cloves, crushed
4 tablespoons oil
2 tomatoes, skinned and chopped
5/8 cup chicken broth
5/8 cup dry white wine
salt and freshly ground black pepper
juice of 1/2 lime
2 teaspoons vinegar
dash of hot pepper sauce

Fry the onion, bell peppers, and garlic in the oil until softened. Add the tomatoes,

stir well and cook for 2 to 3 minutes. Add the broth and wine and cook over medium heat for about 15 minutes, until thickened, stirring occasionally. Season to taste with salt and pepper, and add the lime juice, vinegar, and a dash of hot pepper sauce. Serve with fish, meat, or chicken. Serves 4 to 6

AVOCADO SAUCE

1 large ripe avocado
1 tablespoon finely chopped onion
1 garlic clove, crushed
cayenne pepper, to taste

Halve and peel the avocado, remove the seed and mash the flesh to a smooth paste. Beat in the onion and garlic and season with cayenne pepper. Serve immediately with chicken, fish, and rice dishes. The sauce cannot be prepared in advance as it will discolor if left standing for any length of time, although adding a little lemon juice will help retain the pale green color. Serves 4

PEANUT SAUCE

2 tablespoons shredded onion
2 tablespoons olive oil
2 tablespoons dark brown sugar
1 teaspoon lime juice
2 tablespoons peanut butter
6 tablespoons coconut cream
pinch of salt

Fry the onion gently in the oil until softened, and then stir in the brown sugar, lime juice, and peanut butter. Add the coconut cream, a little at a time, stirring well. Season with salt and cook gently over low heat until the sauce is thick and smooth. Serve with grilled meat and chicken. Serves 4.

BANANA CHUTNEY

12 bananas
1 pound dates, stoned
1 pound green apples, peeled and cored
2 pounds onions
1 cup candied stem ginger, chopped
1 teaspoon ground allspice
2 teaspoons curry powder
1 tablespoon salt
2^1/$_2$ cups vinegar
1^1/$_4$ cups molasses
1^1/$_4$ cups water

Peel and chop the bananas, chop the dates, and thinly slice the apples and onions. Place in an ovenproof dish with the remaining ingredients and stir well. Cook in a preheated oven at 300°F for 2 hours, until thickened. Bottle the banana chutney in sterilized jars and seal. Store in a cool, dark place. Serve with hot curries and grilled and jerked meats. Makes 2 to 3 jars

COCONUT CREAM

1 fresh coconut
hot water

Break open the coconut and remove the flesh. Shred coarsely and add an equal quantity of hot water (1 tablespoon water to every tablespoon of coconut). Let stand for 30 minutes and then strain through cheesecloth into a bowl. The strained liquid is the coconut cream. Use in curries, spicy dishes, and sauces.

PAPAYA SAUCE

2 pounds ripe papayas
1 teaspoon curry powder
1 tablespoon sugar
2 tablespoons lime juice
salt, to taste

Peel and halve the papayas and remove the seeds. Purée the flesh in a blender or food processor. Transfer the puréed papaya to a small saucepan and add the curry powder and sugar. Simmer over very low heat for 10 to 15 minutes, and then stir in the lime juice and salt. Cool and store in a sealed container in the refrigerator for 2 to 3 days. Serve with broiled seafood and chicken. Serves 4

MIXED FRUIT CORDIAL

6 tablespoons sugar
6 tablespoons water
juice of 4 large oranges
juice of 2 lemons
juice of 2 grapefruit
iced water or iced soda water
lemon or lime slices, to serve

Boil the sugar and water for 2 minutes and then set aside to cool. Strain the fruit juices and chill for at least 2 hours. Sweeten to taste with the sugar syrup and then dilute with iced water or iced soda water. Serve the fruit cordial in glasses, garnished with lemon or lime slices. Serves 4 to 6

HOT CHILE OIL

1 hot chile, e.g. Scotch bonnet
^{1}/$_2$ small onion, finely chopped
1 garlic clove, crushed
1 sprig of thyme
2 to 3 chives
2^1/$_2$ cups olive oil

Remove the seeds from the chile and chop the flesh finely. Put into a bottle with the onion, garlic, and herbs. Pour in the olive oil and push in the stopper tightly. Store in a dark, cool place for at least a week before using in marinades for broiled meat, chicken, and fish. Makes 2^1/$_2$ cups

BARBADOS SEASONING

1 onion, finely chopped
2 garlic cloves, crushed
1 tablespoon chopped chives
2 scallions, finely chopped
1 fresh red chile, seeded and finely chopped
1 teaspoon fresh thyme
2 allspice berries, crushed
^{1}/$_2$ teaspoon salt
1 tablespoon lime juice

Pound all the ingredients together in a mortar or process in a blender or food processor. Store the Barbados Seasoning paste either in a screwtop jar or in a sealed container in the refrigerator and use for seasoning scored fish or chicken before broiling or cooking over hot coals on a barbecue.

INDEX